MOVING REFLECTIONS

MOVING REFLECTIONS

a play by Francis Warner

Τεκνία μου . . .

OXFORD THEATRE TEXTS 7

COLIN SMYTHE, GERRARDS CROSS, 1983

British Library Cataloguing in Publication Data

Warner, Francis
Moving reflections.—(Oxford theatre texts,
ISSN 0141–1152; 7)
I. Title   II. Series
822′.914   PR6073.A/

ISBN 0–86140–165–4

First published in 1983 by Colin Smythe Ltd.
Gerrards Cross, Buckinghamshire

Distributed in North America by Humanities Press Inc.
Atlantic Highlands, N.J. 07716

Cover design by John Piper

Produced in Great Britain

FOR GEORGINA

MOVING REFLECTIONS was commissioned for performance in St Giles' Cathedral, Edinburgh by the Oxford University Players and was first performed on Friday, 13th August, 1982. It was directed by Guy Andrews.

The cast was as follows:

ACT ONE		ACT TWO
John	*Jeremy Davies*	
Tiberius	*Brett Hannam*	Prologue
Philo	*Julian Waite*	Ignatius
Christ	*Nicholas Growse*	Pliny
Mary Virgin	*Celia Hill*	
Mary Magdalene	*Caroline Thomas*	
Mary Clopas	*Lesley Kirk*	Domitilla
Soldier & Prologue	*Stephen Brown*	Polycarp
Longinus	*Simon Hardy*	Nicetes
High Priest	*Nicholas Mirzoeff*	Burrhus
	Jane Clutterbuck	Alke

Production Manager Nicholas Vincent. Stage Managers Clare Shine, Ewan Cameron. Lighting Design David Colmer. Chief Electrician Richard Cooper. Sound Paul Barrett. Wardrobe Hazel Sparks. Technical Director Christopher Vile. Posters and book cover designed by John Piper.

Characters

John
Tiberius
Philo
Christ
Mary Virgin
Mary Magdalene
Mary Clopas
Soldier
Longinus
High Priest
Alke
Burrhus
Ignatius
Polycarp
Domitilla
Pliny
Nicetes

Prologues

Act One is set on Capri, and in Jerusalem, at the time of the Crucifixion.

Act Two is set near Ephesus, and in Smyrna, seventy years after Act One.

Act One

Vertiginous where leaping minds have touched
Quickened emotions stripped bare for delight,
We kiss to life the serious faith of John.

SECOND PROLOGUE (JOHN)

Those who reject love find love rejects them,
The full, rich tide thins, swamps, ebbs out, till sharp
Granites of lifelong pain rock pride's ripped craft
As human diminishes, and jaundice swells
Leaning on righteous crutches : 'Pity me ! Pity me !'
To stagger self-condemned, weep in a mirror
Half-lit, rather than say 'Yes ! I was wrong !'
And turn. Such claw flesh from their cheeks and beg,
Cringe for affection, kill where they would curl,
Needle heroin into their mothers' breasts
And jaunt on egg-shell, tip-toe in despair,
Still boasting to ignoring crowds 'I'm right !'
The artery severed and their life-force dead
To evoke from hell this fundamental law —
Our dance of darkness shows light loves.

Act One

Capri.

TIBERIUS *alone.*

TIBERIUS   From here, Capri, my garden island fortress –
Fragrant in spring's first Mediterranean light,
Sweet with the scent of cypress, mist, and vines,
Blossom and pines and myrtle pure as snow
(Though Venus' flower) and all migrating birds
That wing the cliffs one thousand feet below
From Africa, weaving swift threads of silk,
Darting each grotto cool and dark as a shell,
Stroking the waves, to soar and settle high,
Here, on their long flight, till with dawnbreak song
They leave for Europe and the farthest North;
Though not this redbreast — look! pricking my
        finger
He hops and trusts in full throat, Rome's, no doubt,
Bringing the news Sejanus' neck is cut,
Pruned by my gardening letters to the senate :
I, master of the world, Tiberius Caesar,
Princeps, Pontifex Maximus, Administrator
(My proudest title, I disdain all others
Save Poet), from this high Tarpeian rock,
I rule the world bequeathed me by Augustus,
One time my guardian, stepfather, and god,
Augustus Caesar, dead for fifteen years;
And I myself now three score years and ten,
In self-imposed, protective exile, searching
For peace, restless and waiting.
He used to sleep with his hands on his eyes
In this same room, his summer residence,
Mine all year round. Across the bruise-soft sea
Beneath those heights of Cumae there's the cave
Aeneas found in which the foaming-mouthed
Sibyl Deiphobe answered his prayer
Foretelling wars, and Tiber red with blood,
Days come and gone. And yet strange opal words
Sung by our gravest singer, who taught me
When I was young, Virgil : he said that Time,

Pregnant, was bringing to birth a new Apollo,
And all past centuries of hated wars
Will cease, the night of horror end with dawn.
Creation dances in expectancy.
Lion and ox will play in peace; foxgloves,
Smiling acanthus, ivy, Egyptian lilies,
Will shape themselves his petal-pillowed cradle.
Where is this god, forecast when I was born?

PHILO *has entered.*

PHILO   Ah, Caesar, you, who comprehend so much
And know men's eyes seek out this dying world,
Dimming our deeper vision, keener than sight
That weeps to being all that's unforeseen
Unless, blinded by drink and ignorance,
We annex earth and lose eternity,
I know you loved Augustus, and for him
Plucked the iron dragon's teeth beyond the Rhine
Nine times; and Roman Danube idols you,
Makes you its love, because you will not shed
The blood of legions for the bark of swine.
Detail is your delight, and mercy too.
When, in your Triumph, Bato rode in chains
You did not strangle him before the crowds
In Roman custom, but gave him a home,
Mosaic gardens in wind-soft Ravenna.
And since, with tireless generosity
Of heart, your touch has held the world with peace.
In Alexandria I teach the Law
Of Moses, and we Jews, too, love the Greek
Poets as you do—Meleager's Cos,
Theocritus, and sweet Callimachus:
'Delos, wind-swept and battered by the sea,'
Is not unlike your island sanctuary.
We honour, too, your tutor and your friend,
Virgil; and have a prophecy that says
A boy is born whose goodness will be known,
For God has given him strength and thoughtfulness.
The wolf and new-born lamb will share their straw
In friendship, and this little child will lead

The calf and lion, as he shepherds home
All tear-stained cheeks of the far-scattered ones
From the four corners of a world at peace.
None will destroy, or hurt, for, as the sea
Blankets its coral bed to the far ice,
So all mankind will leave its night of vice.

TIBERIUS   My own son, Drusus, died seven years ago
Extinguishing all music in my head,
And though I loved Augustus, he too maimed me :
Gave me Vispania to be my bride
When she was one year old, and I was nine.
Rome's eyes grew soft to watch us play and dance.
She had my adolescent heart, and I
Had her entire devotion. She was me,
Bore me our baby, Drusus. But, when Augustus'
Daughter, his only Julia, became a widow,
He forced me divorce this goddess of night flowers,
The only girl on earth I ever loved,
Took her away, to leave me free for Julia.
My stepfather became my father-in-law.
Julia had a son by me who died,
But I no longer cared.
I saw Vispania across a street
Once, and my tears were such he passed a law
Forbidding her, even by chance, my sight.

PHILO   It's long ago, Tiberius. Was this the reason
Last night you paced the steps beside my room
Until your sandals are what they are now,
Rags round your feet?

TIBERIUS   No.

PHILO   The legions love you. Herod Antipas
Built on the harp-shaped lake of Galilee
Its capital, and gave to it . . . your name.
And Philip, too, beneath Mount Hermon's strength
Right at the source of Jordan, builds a great
City with all the Roman panoply
And, once more, dedicates it to . . . your name.

TIBERIUS   Philo, last night was the worst I have lived,
            And yet I don't know why.

PHILO   Why were you saying Virgil's prophecy
            When I came in?

TIBERIUS   Because it fills my mind.

PHILO   Every good, every wise man has the gift
            Of prophecy.

TIBERIUS   Philo, we both are scholars, you the greater.
            This Greek word 'Logos', which our Stoics call
            The reasoning principle that creates matter,
            Its coded pattern, immanent in all —
            You use the word in a far different sense
            In Alexandria.

PHILO   It's true, we do.
            For us the Logos is not in the world
            At all, but far beyond it, perfect form
            Of our imperfect possibilities
            There realized fresh from the mind of God.
            Think how a beam of light is not its source,
            Nor is it that which it reveals to sight,
            And yet without light nothing is perceived.
            God is the fountain from which water flows
            To nourish earthly life. To us the Logos
            Is water, light, and wisdom.

TIBERIUS   Bear with me
            A moment. Say, just say, that once in Time,
            As Virgil and your own Isaiah sing,
            That go-between became embodied in
            Not light, nor water, but one living man?
            And, as I loved my Drusus, God loved him;
            And he died, murdered, as my Drusus was.
            Can you imagine, though no Emperor
            As I am, what the creator of the world,
            The archetype of which I am the copy,
            Might feel; might do?

PHILO   Caesar, now, for the first time in my life,
               I feel a weight of spiritual fear
               And you are teaching me. Please stop. No more.

               Thunder.

TIBERIUS   No rain? I dread the thunder. But you must
               Know what I feel, and what kept me awake
               This night now passing into blackened day.
               God would become a Stoic, and the Logos
               From now on would indeed become the code
               Inherent in all matter; nothing else :
               A formula soon to be found by man,
               Who being evil to the very core
               Will turn it on itself, the secret found
               And harnessed will become the plaything, boast
               Of power politics, and one sick day
               Some petty Caesar will blow up the earth.

               Sound of storm wind in background. No rain.

PHILO   No more. Your Drusus' death has made you mad.

TIBERIUS   I seldom lose my temper, Philo, least
               Of all with you; but get out of my sight.
               I tell you, in the marrow of my bones
               I feel the earth quake, but can't understand!
               What madman has unleashed Pandora's box,
               What blasphemy pours dark across the world?
               Philo, I am not mad. The Altar of Peace
               Sits on my desk, a copy of that in Rome
               Carved by Greek workmen. Look! The sky's
                    eclipsed!
               Go on your journey to Jerusalem;
               And when hot Egypt beckons you again,
               Visit me once more on your voyage home.

PHILO   The urge to know God is the gift of God,
               That is his revelation to us here.
               The Logos never could be one frail man;
               Only in metaphor is it God's son.
               Tiberius, the closed eye of the soul

Can open again; for, as Cleanthes sang,
The Logos is not Zeus's thunderbolt,
God can make perfect even monstrous things.
I do not know what has disturbed your mind,
Nor do I know why pollen of despair
Hangs in the air.
I'll leave, and on return from Palestine
Bring you whatever little news is mine.

SCENE TWO

Jerusalem. Cross, with actor playing CHRIST *nailed
to it.* LONGINUS *the centurion near, by him a large
bowl of sour wine.* MARY VIRGIN *standing,* MARY
CLOPAS *kneeling with forehead on ground. Both
Marys have their shoes off. Enter to them* MARY
MAGDALENE.

MARY CLOPAS   You've come.

MAGDALENE   How did it happen?

MARY CLOPAS   After supper.
He went into Gethsemane to pray.

MAGDALENE   Is that where Judas . . . ?

MARY CLOPAS   Yes. Temple police
Crossed over Kedron valley to the garden
With swords and clubs, encircled him, and tied
His hands behind his back.

MAGDALENE   Lamb to the slaughter.

MARY CLOPAS   He never raised his voice. The menfolk fled.
Annas was waiting with his wolves at home.

MAGDALENE   Annas! What, that old man? He has no power.

MARY CLOPAS   He used it though.

MAGDALENE   That ex-High Priest thrown out
And mocked by Pontius Pilate's predecessor
Valerius Gratus?

MARY CLOPAS   True, no legal power.
It was illegally, without a charge,
No witness for defence — our basic right —
At full moon in mock trial they found him guilty.

MAGDALENE   Guilty of what?

MARY CLOPAS   The dogs had closed in on him.
Nothing, at this stage. Later, blasphemy.

MAGDALENE   There is no trace of perjury in him,
And he has done no violence! He is punished
For our iniquities.

MARY CLOPAS   Speak for yourself.
Daybreak today the full Sanhedrin met
With Caiaphas, Annas' own son-in-law,
And legalized the horror of the night.
At their request, Pilate examined him
And found him innocent — yet had him
               scourged . . .

MAGDALENE   Scourged!

MARY CLOPAS   Yes, no doubt of that.

MAGDALENE   He's had no sleep!
Why have they wound that branch around his
               head?

MARY CLOPAS   They tortured him, while Pilate washed his hands,
Knowing him innocent. 'Look at your king!'
Yes, Pilate mocked us Jews. 'We have no king
But Caesar! Send him to be crucified!'
The sneering weakling gave the mob lynch law.

MAGDALENE	(*Catching sight of* MARY VIRGIN, *who has collapsed*) Mary! (*Going to her*) Help me lift her up!
JOHN	(*To* MARY VIRGIN) Come, hold my arms. (*They look up*) The sky is turning black!
JESUS	Mother, accept your son. Son, take your mother.
JOHN	I will. (*To* MARY) You've seen enough; can bear no more. (*Leading her away. To* MAGDALENE *and* MARY CLOPAS) The final moments will be unbearable For her. I'll take her home, and then come back. (*Exeunt*)
MAGDALENE	We'll stay.

Lights down to denote passing of time. Muffled drums.

JESUS	(*Weakly*) I'm thirsty.
SOLDIER	*Stands up, throws down dice with which he has been playing, plucks some sprigs of hyssop from a bush, and slowly walks over to* LONGINUS. *He borrows his javelin, ties the sprigs to the end of it, dips it in wine, and then carefully reaches up to sprinkle* JESUS's *face, and let him sip a leaf.* JOHN *returns, and not understanding why the* SOLDIER *is holding a javelin to* JESUS's *face is shocked at first, but restrained by* MARY CLOPAS *before he can interfere, as the* SOLDIER's *obvious gentleness is completed.* SOLDIER *then returns javelin to* LONGINUS, *and stands by him.*
JESUS	(*Loud voice*) It is finished!
LONGINUS	(*To* SOLDIER) There is no doubt this was the Son of God.

Blackout.

SCENE THREE

MAGDALENE I spend my nights crying. Tears are on my cheeks
             when I wake.
           No-one can comfort us now.
           Jerusalem, built on two hills, surrounded with honey
             walls,
           You have become a criminal; your dress drags in
             the dirt.
           In the souk little children sigh standing in open
             places.
           Does it mean nothing to you who pass by? Has
             there ever been anguish like mine?
           Our too-much-loved city degraded; our music and
             laughter silenced.
           Even the sun is eclipsed. An earthquake has
             shattered the Temple.
           Was this the perfection of cities, the joy of the
             whole earth?
           Now women abort on benches and there is no-one
             to help.
           The cats and dogs will be eaten. The sucking child's
             tongue turns black.
           We drink our own water: there is nothing to fill
             our breasts.
           My dancing is lost to grief, my long hair matted
             with sorrow.
           Oh God, oh God, come and help me! The joy of
             my heart has died.
           (*To audience*) Does it matter so little to you that
             our city of peace has committed
           Consciously, with false law, smeared with the cant
             of religion,
           The murder of Goodness on earth?
           And now they have taken my Lord, and I don't
             know where they have put him.
           Wasn't his life enough for your cruelty? Couldn't
             you leave us his corpse, just his body?

           CHRIST *has entered behind her, and she becomes
           aware of him.*

You, sir, if you have seen any soldiers or priests
    while gardening,
Taking away our friend, tell me where they have
    laid him?

CHRIST   Mary.

MAGDALENE   (*Turning to him*) Rabbuni! (*Drops on knees about
to clasp his feet*)

CHRIST   You may not touch me now, because I have not yet
        ascended;
But go and tell the others that I am ascending to
        My Father
        And your Father,
        My God
        And your God.   (*Exit*)

MAGDALENE   (*Pause*) *I have seen him!* (*Runs off*)

SCENE FOUR

JOHN   Has Peter come?

MARY CLOPAS   No. You look out of breath.

JOHN   It's true! I raced him there and then peeped in
But saw the linen grave-clothes lying flat!

MARY CLOPAS   Flat?

JOHN   Yes! The layers of upper winding-sheet
Had fallen in on top of the lower ones.

MARY CLOPAS   You mean . . .

JOHN   Yes. Right! Collapsed in on itself.
No-one has stolen the body; if they had,
The linen strips in which the corpse was bound —

And really tightly bound, because those wounds
Were still slow-bleeding — would be missing too!

MARY CLOPAS   Then what has happened?

JOHN   Where is James? I must find my elder brother!
The body has passed through the winding-sheets!
Even the napkin binding his thorned head
Lies just a neck-space from the body-cloths
Exactly as though the head has disappeared
Like air : the burial bandage has fallen in
On empty space!

MARY CLOPAS   Oh mighty God! (*Pause*) You know how he loved
the psalms,
And was always quoting them?

JOHN   (*Both now highly excited*) That crossed my mind!
He was even saying them while on the cross.

MARY CLOPAS   'Thou shalt not leave my soul in Sheol . . .'

JOHN   'Neither shalt thou
Suffer thy Holy One to see corruption.'

MARY CLOPAS   Of course God couldn't let him decompose!
And now, so much is clearer; things he said :
'Let not your heart be troubled, neither let
It be afraid . . .'

JOHN   'In a little while the world will no longer see me;
But you will see me. Because I live, you will too.'

MARY CLOPAS   'I will not leave you desolate.'

Enter MARY MAGDALENE.

MAGDALENE   I have seen him! I have talked to him,
And so has Peter!

CHRIST   Peace be with you.

Blackout.

SCENE FIVE

Two voices heard in blackout; one, that of the
HIGH PRIEST, *the other that of* PETER.

VOICE ONE   We gave you an injunction not to preach
                The name of Jesus; and what have you done?
                Filled all Jerusalem with resurrection,
                And nail the guilt of this man's death on us.

VOICE TWO   Obedience to God comes before man.

SCENE SIX

*Growing hubbub of angry voices, then fade to
silence. Lights up on* JOHN, *fresh from having been
scourged, and* MARY VIRGIN, *dressing his wounds.*

MARY VIRGIN   Just talk and talk. Tell me what they did.

JOHN   My father would not stay to watch his son
                Lashed in the synagogue in front of friends,
                Loathed by the whole Sanhedrin; but my tutor,
                Philo, who only reached this City of Peace
                Last night, sat by Gamaliel, his host,
                And watched both Peter and myself spat on,
                Mouthed at for execution. Gamaliel
                With all the sadness of his life at law
                Sweetened their bitterness; talked of Hillel,
                And won some Pharisees to gentle us
                With thirty-nine incisions of the lash.

MARY VIRGIN   Poor and dear Peter. What did Philo say?

JOHN   He was a guest and kept his dignity
                With silence; like your son : I wish they'd met!

When at the thirty-eighth I split my knees
And looked up, on his cheek was one sharp tear
That caught the light. He knew, and turned away.

MARY VIRGIN   I think Gamaliel does understand;
And Nicodemus; and Arimathea.
Perhaps, too, Philo will? How does that feel?

JOHN   (*In pain*) Ah! Dearest Mother, thank you. No, no
       more.
I'm well enough to talk of something else.
Pain makes me concentrate just on myself.
Mary, you married so young; tell me, when
Did you learn Greek?

MARY VIRGIN   (*Laughs*) John! Not too young. Trembling
Just on the brink of womanhood, before
I had lost blood. Yes, I was twelve years old,
According to our normal Jewish custom,
When I was given by my beloved father
To quiet Joseph as his future bride.

JOHN   And then?

MARY VIRGIN   And then? Yes, it was that same year
Jesus was born.

JOHN   You never talk of your son as a baby
Kicking inside you as most mothers do.

MARY VIRGIN   John, yes I will, but not today. Few things
Can be more private than what came to me
In that miraculous year of our engagement.
You asked when I learned Greek? Once we were
      married,
Joseph and I took our baby away to Egypt
Because of Herod's mad infanticide
In Bethlehem and villages around.
Once we had settled (as you will have found
Now you're an undergraduate yourself
In Egypt's Alexandria) no-one could speak

Our native Aramaic. To buy a melon,
Or make new friends with other teenage mothers,
Greek was the only language. Yes, the soldiers
Speak Latin, but Greek is the common talk.
Even your tutor, Philo — and you are lucky
To have him as your tutor — our greatest scholar
Of Jewish law and God's philosophy,
Can read no Hebrew.

JOHN   He speaks and writes pure Greek,
And all our Hebrew scriptures reads translated
Into the language Socrates enhanced
And eye-dark Homer sang.

MARY VIRGIN   And we shall use.
Now; would you like to share what you have
    written?
Or shall we leave it, modesting these wounds?

JOHN   (*Taking up parchments*) Mary, correct me ruth-
    lessly. You know
What I am like. I've only started Greek
At university, so mine is narrow,
And specialized. Yes, Zebedee, my father,
Is rich enough with his proud fishing-fleet
To send me away to study, but in vacation
He makes me sail with his professionals,
And when I get impatient, shouts me down :
'Oh, you're well named sudden Boanerges,
My quick-tempered, impatient son of thunder!'
And I yell : 'Right! Like father, man, like son!'
And then he laughs; or sometimes knocks me down.

MARY VIRGIN   (*Playfully*) He keeps you shore-bound, mending nets.
    The first
Teacher who comes along distracts you from
Your father's chores!

JOHN   At least it was your son,
And so your fault. Be strict with me, and if
My style is weak, or if the thought's one-sided,
Correct me. Here's a start : (*Reads in rhetorical
manner*)

'That which was from the beginning, which we have heard, which we have seen with our eyes, which we have looked upon, and our hands have handled, of the Word of Life . . .'

MARY VIRGIN   Why don't you just say
'We tell you what we have seen and heard'?

JOHN   Ah, yes. That's better. (*Pause*) Right! I'll start with that.

MARY VIRGIN   God is light, and in him is no darkness at all.

JOHN   Yes, but now to the point.
'If we say we are his and walk in darkness, we lie.'

MARY   I should have thought the point was that if we Acknowledge our sins, he will forgive us?

JOHN   Absolutely!
'If we say we've not sinned we make God a liar.'

MARY VIRGIN   Must you? This is what he used to say:
'He that loves his brother lives in light and won't stumble.'

JOHN   That's not enough! We must put the other side — And a reference. For instance:
'Not like Cain, who belonged to Satan and slit his brother's sacrificial throat. And why? To make the crops grow and because he was evil, jealous of his brother's goodness.' (*With increasing enthusiasm*) Better still! 'He that hates his brother lives in darkness, and walks in darkness, and doesn't know where he is going, because darkness has blinded his eyes.'

MARY VIRGIN   John; don't you sometimes feel . . . ? Never mind.

JOHN   'If you refuse love you become dead inside,
                        And whoever is like that is a murderer;
                        And you know no murderer has eternal life
                        In him.'

MARY VIRGIN   Can't we just say 'Little children,
                        Love one another'?

JOHN   Naïve! That's not enough!

MARY VIRGIN   I'm thinking of this letter being read
                        By friends, and all my son's close followers.
                        Look. Write this down; from me:
                            'My little children, if any one sins, we have an
                        advocate with God the Father, in Jesus. He is the
                        sacrifice willing to suffer for us, and take away not
                        only our shortcomings, but the sins of the whole
                        world.'

JOHN   (*Feeling slightly chastened*) Ah! The world! How's
                        this?
                            'All that is in the world, the lust (*with relish*) of the
                        flesh, the lust of the eyes, and the pride of life, is
                        not of the Father. We know that we are of God,
                        and the whole world lies in wickedness . . .'

MARY VIRGIN   (*Amused and gentle*) Steady, your wounds will open.
                            May I finish?

JOHN   (*Still carried away*)
                        'And he that commits sin is of the Devil.'

MARY VIRGIN   (*Smiling*) You baby! Listen.
                            'If our heart condemns us, God is greater than our
                        hearts, and knows everything. And if our conscience
                        does not condemn us, then we need not be afraid
                        in God's presence.'

JOHN   What of the other side? Of deadly sin?

MARY VIRGIN   We know he hears us, whatever we may ask.

JOHN   Yes! but surely some sins are unforgivable?

MARY VIRGIN   Really?

JOHN   You have a fatal habit of seeing
Good all the time. It's far more complicated.
'There is sin not deadly, but there is deadly sin.

Knock at door.

You shall pray for one, and not pray for the other.
There are three that bear witness in Heaven :
          the Father, the Word
(Or the Logos), the Holy Ghost; and these three
          are one.
And there are three that bear witness on earth . . .'
Is that someone at the door?

MARY VIRGIN   I think it is. Just add this note, and end.
'Little children,
Don't worry over technicalities.'

                    SCENE SEVEN

*Angry crowd outside, slow hand-clapping in unison
becoming faster, voices increasing in excitement till
climax on wild peals of laughter from the crowd.
Repeat.*

JOHN   Philo!

MARY VIRGIN   I'm glad you've come.

PHILO   Mary, I had
Not thought we two would ever meet. For me
The quest is joy enough. To hold you here
And share your company brings almost too great
Awareness what one single human has
Contained within herself and brought to birth.
Your beauty is not like the summer's sky
But incorruptible.

MARY VIRGIN   I reflect a light
Of which I am not the source.

PHILO   Irradiated
By that full rainbow of which we are half.

MARY VIRGIN   It happened in time, with eternal consequence.
History is different now.

PHILO   You are the ruby
Fired with giving thanks to God, but I —
Pale with perplexity and pilgrimage —
Only the opal. John, you are in pain.

JOHN   Mary has bathed my wounds, and we have written
A letter you must read. Listen! Outside!
What bloodlust drives our Laestrygonians?
Whose ship of life is bouldered from its berth?

PHILO   That new Ulysses is your own friend, Stephen.
The xenophobic, Aramaic Temple
Priests detest your Greek-tongued, charismatic
Pooler of property, their sharpest critic,
A man who mixes with sons of freed slaves
Brought here from Alexandria by Pompey
One hundred years ago. The Temple loathes
Foreigners' synagogues, the Septuagint,
All that deflects cash and content away
From Sanhedrin and primogeniture.

MARY VIRGIN   What has our Stephen done?

PHILO   The charge? The same
By which your son was cruelly condemned.
We must stay here, lock ourselves in, and wait,
For outside chaos climbs.

MARY VIRGIN   They die for blasphemy that tell the truth,
And those late winter weeds choke our fresh spring,
Crowd down our buds till colours stain the earth.

Yet, from the blood of love a new world grows.
We have a knowledge nothing can destroy.
Death's dark's dispelled, first light breaks from
        the grave,
And Egypt's pyramids are worthless trash.
Time is newborn as grace dissolves fear's frost,
For now eternal life has come at last.

JOHN   We must go out and help him!

PHILO   They want you.
Listen! The High Priest is about to calm
The crowd, and speak.

JOHN   Mary, he'd kill us all.

MARY VIRGIN   The almond blossom, January pink
And white, comes long before its pointed leaves,
And later still the dark nut white with oil.
Our wind anemone's own crimson blush
Touches our eyes each year after the first
And early rain, weeks before Passover.
John, John. A sword will pierce your own heart,
        too.
But, from the blood that fell from Jesus' side,
And from the wounds your suffering has borne,
The purple life soon to leave Stephen's veins
And those of crowds of joyful witnesses
As yet to come, in countries still unborn,
There will rise up, beyond our Jewish race,
Above the wealth of Greece and reach of Rome,
A new humanity beloved of Christ.
We are its birth, its spring.

JOHN   How will they know?

PHILO   You must write down all you have known, and seen.

MARY VIRGIN   And I will help you.

SCENE EIGHT

Dark. Spotlight on HIGH PRIEST *standing alone.*

HIGH PRIEST   So we, the guardians of Mosaic Law,
The Temple-keepers of the Ark of God,
Have killed the prophets? Are idolaters?
'The Most High does not live in temples built
With human hands . . .' What insolence! We hold
The precious centre of our Jewish faith
In sacred trust for coming generations
Even as Solomon bequeathed it us
Upon a hill, surrounded by a wall.
Great Herod took away our old foundations
To order fresh, one hundred cubits long,
Each stone twenty-five cubits, white and strong.
All's now encircled by great cloisters, while
A golden vine in the centre tears men's sight
As it spreads out under the crown-work, branches
Hanging from a great height. This was grave error
In our religion? No! Our pride and life.
We have apostatized the Law, the gift
Of angels? Killed the Holy One, Messiah?
Understood nothing of God's Israel?
This is black blasphemy and revolution.
You, who despise our ritual purity,
Would mock our customs, tear our Temple down,
Shall die by stones beside this city wall.

A cheer from the crowd.

Enter MARY CLOPAS. *She climbs high to look out of window.*

MARY CLOPAS   The witnesses are throwing the first stones
But they are falling short. Oh God, God save him!
They're using builders' rubble. He's on his knees,
He's turned this way, near me. Yes! I can hear!
He's telling us: 'I see high Heaven open!'
He's smiling, looking up; his face transfigured.

'I can see Heaven open now on high,
The Son of Man standing on the right hand
Of God.' They put their fingers in their ears
And savage him with rocks.

(*Great shout from crowd. Then silence*)

JOHN   Why are they silent?

MARY CLOPAS He's dead. No. No! He's not! What is he saying?
He commends his soul to God as your son did,
And asks forgiveness for his murderers.

MARY VIRGIN It's over?

MARY CLOPAS   Yes.

They pray silently.

SCENE NINE

PHILO   John, this may be the last time that we meet.

MARY CLOPAS Only you will be left to write it down.

MARY VIRGIN John. While our Stephen's blood spreads on the
                 ground
And we wait for the knock upon the door
We shall all start you on your golden book.

JOHN   I will begin with Genesis' first words. (*Writing*)

MARY CLOPAS 'In the beginning . . .'

MARY VIRGIN   Perfect. Philo, teach us —
You wisest scholar in our Jewish world
And John's own tutor — teach us how to tell
Our loved one's story in immortal words.

JOHN   Let this cup be our prayer for inspiration.
                Philo, that wisdom that you shared with Caesar —
                What was it you two greatest men discussed?

PHILO   I did not understand it then as now,
                And still all is not clear. Mary, I need
                Your guidance; and yours, John. You know far
                    more
                Deeply than I do; you have seen the truth.
                A tutor can but lead you by the hand,
                Prepare your spirit and inform your thoughts.
                He cannot force the spark leap from the dark
                Or bring illumination down from God.
                In the beginning was the Logos, Word.
                To find the Father of this universe
                Is, as our Plato said, a most hard task.
                Yet order, and the beauty of the stars,
                The plants and generative seeds of life,
                Fill us with awe and wonder at God's work,
                Confirm our knowledge of his sleepless mind,
                Wake in us joy, and make us restless till
                Those new, fresh, blessèd thoughts of ageless God
                Call us back to him.

MARY VIRGIN   Philo, teach us words
                As cousin John, our Baptist; give us manna
                Clean, clear, transparent for our aching minds.

JOHN   In the beginning was the Word. (*Writing*)

PHILO   With God,
                And of God. And the world was made by him.

MARY CLOPAS   In him is life; his life the light of men

JOHN   Shining in darkness darkness cannot grasp.

PHILO   His son, perfect in virtue, is our pleader
                For our forgiveness, and for the supply
                Of God's ungrudging benefits. We love
                Him if we follow Moses' Law.

MARY CLOPAS   No, No!
                That is impersonal; the rabbis' way!

MARY VIRGIN   Yes. We love him because he first loved us.

PHILO   To Greeks, Logos is Mind expressing itself;
                For Jews it is the Word of God come down.
                God is himself unknowable.

MARY CLOPAS   He has
                Revealed himself in Jesus' broken tomb.

MARY VIRGIN   The Word was made flesh, of my virgin body.
                He lived among us, and we saw his glory
                As it was; full of joy, and grace, and truth.

JOHN   This Word, this Logos, incarnate in flesh,
                Unites both Moses and the wisest Greeks.
                I must find James to help me. Where is he?
                My elder brother could write this so well!

MARY CLOPAS   He was with Stephen. Then he disappeared.

MARY VIRGIN   He was with Peter, who too disappeared.

                Pause.

JOHN   (*Slowly beginning to write again*) All who believe,
                        all who receive his name,
                He gives them power to be the Sons of God.

PHILO   Reason extends now as a living breath
                Through every portion of the universe,
                The ground of human nature, and your Jesus
                Is teaching this is nothing less than love?

                              SCENE TEN

                Knocking. Enter MARY MAGDALENE.

MAGDALENE   There comes a time, on the far side of grief
                And joy, when my emotions will not function.

My prayers fly crooked up to Heaven, my tears
Fall to the ground empty of grief, and dry.
Your brother James is dead. To please the Temple
Herod's beheaded him. As next of kin
His guard send you this basket with his head.

PHILO   The claws are closing in. John, you are next.
Lady, I come from old Tiberius
And I have wealth. At my expense go to him,
Stand face to face with Caesar. He will see you
Alone, at my request. Tell him of all
This family has known. Of resurrection
From the grave. Above all of her son.
Though he will listen, he may not believe,
But try. Tell him of Herod's carnage here;
Of Pontius Pilate's crimes and silver palm.
Go to Capri. And Mary, John, you all,
Escape now — to Samaria; then on
To Ephesus when old Tiberius dies.
That viper nurtured by Rome's lupine dugs
To follow him as the next Emperor,
Caligula, will be our enemy.
Sail for Capri while wisdom still rules Rome.

MARY VIRGIN   Your beauty will remind Tiberius
Of days long gone, of heartache long ago.
Do not prepare what you shall say to him.
Just trust in God.

MARY CLOPAS   Philo, protect our girl.

JOHN   I will go with her!

PHILO   No. A brother's grief
Must drive you on to write the divine book.

MARY VIRGIN   Come, let us bury our loved ones in Christ;
Then leave for Philip in Samaria.

SCENE ELEVEN

Capri. TIBERIUS *alone.*

TIBERIUS   These cliffs, these softest breezes on my cheeks,
I love them as they soothe my ruffled bed
By lamplight as dawn breaks. I cannot sleep
While the long letter to the Senate lies
Unfinished on my table. It is easy,
Too easy, to destroy; but to create
As our great architect of empire did,
Augustus, is a miracle. Men's hearts
Are savage. However spurious their loves,
At least their hatreds can be counted on.
Am I transformed, deranged by total power,
As men say? No. Saddened. My solitude
They misconstrue debauchery. At my age!
The dawn voice of the sea! (*Writing*) 'Herewith
    I banish
Actors from Rome; they fornicate the women
And stir up riots.' Paulina has been fooled,
Her chastity violated? A lovesick youth?
What's this? 'Bribed priests enticed her overnight
Into the Temple of Isis? Decius Mundus
Dressed in a dog's head, calling himself Anubis,
Enjoyed her all night long? Her husband's stained?'
Those old priests shall be crucified. Their temple
Demolished. Their wooden statue of Isis thrown
Into the Tiber. Mundus is banished. (*Writes*) At
    least
He loved. Oh Rome, Rome, Rome!
Hectic and sprawling megalopolis;
I am as stern with myself as with you.
No, I will not accept your fawning gifts
Of flattery; and senators, why, why
Abase yourselves, offer me empty titles:
'The Father of us all'; a shrine — such baubles?
Should I, who broke the greatest nations, and
Declined so many Triumphs in my youth,
Bend to the foolish crown of a suburban

Parade in my old age? The fact, not dress,
Of power preoccupies my darkening mind.
The weight and care of service to the state,
The Empire, and not least the provinces,
You should share with me. But you cringe; defer
To me, and go home early. Read this, loud,
To the full Senate : 'Every Senator
Must work full hours. No one may be condemned
To death without a ten-day interim
So I can sanction or reprieve.' We must
Conserve, continue and build this great work
Of world peace. Compromise, commodity,
Those twin gold eagles of the Roman State
Are not enough. (*Writing*) 'If I knew what to write,
To you at this time, or what not to write,
Senators, may heaven plunge me in
Worse ruin than I feel now overwhelms
Me every day . . .' (*Writes*)

SCENE TWELVE

MAGDALENE   Caesar?

TIBERIUS   Are you a ghost?

MAGDALENE   No. Just a girl too terrified to speak.

TIBERIUS   How strange you should appear here with the dawn;
Your freshness set against the open sea,
And there, behind your head, slowly appearing,
The grey-white peaks of sun-touched Apennines
Reflecting in the water. Is the guard
Neglecting my protection? He shall die.

MAGDALENE   No. You left word that I should be admitted
When I arrived. I've come to you from Philo.

TIBERIUS   Who are you? And where from? You, you disturb
Some memories in me that I had hoped
Were blasted from my mind. Why are you here?

You have not come to kill me; but your presence
Carries authority you cannot bear.
Why are you crying?

MAGDALENE   I don't know what to say!

TIBERIUS   Lady; I loved a girl strangely like you,
She stood in the same way. She was my bride.
Tell me, why do you shiver in your tears?

MAGDALENE   I had prepared so many things to say
And now I have forgotten them . . . (*Breaks down*)

TIBERIUS   Come, come.
Can I remember my Theocritus?
'The cocks were heralding for the third time
The break of dawn. Can I appear snub-nosed,
Dear nymph, when seen up close? A bearded satyr?'

MAGDALENE   (*Laughing through tears*) I'm sorry. Oh Caesar,
                    though I have seen God
I was not frightened as I am with you.

TIBERIUS   You have seen God?

MAGDALENE   Yes. That is why I'm here.
Jesus, our loved one, when I was too ill
To move, healed me; loved with the purest love.
He suffered crucifixion under Pilate,
And his own family and loyal friends
(Of whom I am the least, and the most grateful)
Despaired. But he has risen from the dead!
I know they sound wild words, but would I be
Here now, have faced the horrors of the voyage,
If what I tell you had not many times
Been tested and found true? The Son of God
Died, and was raised again; talked, ate with us,
And life will never be the same again.

TIBERIUS   There's something in your words I wish were
                    true . . .

MAGDALENE   It is ! Oh Caesar, do you ever pray?

TIBERIUS   I pray that I may live and rule only
                So long as is advantage to the State.

MAGDALENE   I mean with joy ! With certainty and love?

TIBERIUS   The long vicissitudes of army life
                Have left me with a sense unshakeable
                Of what self-killed Lucretius called the tragic
                Seriousness and tears of human life.

MAGDALENE   But look ! God loves the world, and gave his Son,
                His only Son, so that whoever loves
                Him shall not perish but have everlasting
                Life beyond death !

TIBERIUS   Blessing or horror ? Which ?
                Look, beauty; I, too, tried to love the world.
                In Rome, when I was seventeen, defended
                King Archelaus of Cappadocia,
                Rich men of Tralles, and Thessalians :
                Alone, before the Senate, pleaded the Emperor's
                Remission of tribute to those suffering
                Earthquake and natural catastrophe
                In Thyatira, Chios, Laodicea.
                Now once again, I, near the end of life,
                Can and do remit taxes, send my wealth
                To relieve famine in the flooded cities
                Of Asia — and order an ex-praetor,
                With five picked lictors to preside over
                Disaster rehabilitation there.
                Here lies grim satisfaction of great strength :
                To do some little good before I go,
                And hand a stable State (in spite of gangrene
                Frailty of humans) on to my successor,
                All its administrative bones secure.

MAGDALENE   Oh Caesar, how can I begin to know
              Your world? I am a simple Jewish girl
              From Magdala. You saw its watch-tower once.
              You visited our new Tiberias;
              Named after you.

TIBERIUS   You have effect on me.
              We live, as Plato taught, our earthly life
              Inside a fire-lit cave, in which we see
              Only the shadows of reality,
              Moving reflections, prisoned in our flesh.
              Only beyond death can we reach the air
              And see, leaving perplexity behind,
              The sun itself, the goodness we have sought
              In vain below.

MAGDALENE   Jesus was in that cave,
              Buried, sealed in, a Roman guard on watch.
              And yet he broke, like pannag through the soil,
              Out of death's dark dominion!

TIBERIUS   Pannag? Bread?
              And there is Pontius Pilate's lack of judgement
              Again! I have great pride that on my coins
              Are stamped two words: one, Moderation;
              The other, Clemency. I shall show none
              To Pilate. He'll be cashiered of command
              And stand right here. Is this what you desire?

MAGDALENE   Caesar, whatever you command shall be.
              Only — protect our sprig of Christian faith.
              (Christians are what they call us.) You'll be blest
              More than for all your mighty works and days
              For this one act.

TIBERIUS   I will. The Senate shall
              Receive with this imperial letter word
              That Caesar votes in favour of your Jesus:
              And my grey anger will admit no light
              Against accusers of the Christians.

MAGDALENE   If you, Tiberius, were just a man
I'd hug you.

TIBERIUS   No. You make me weep. In fifty
Years no tears have stained my cheeks ! Go home.
Go from this room ! The master of the world
Bows to your Christ.

Fade.

END OF ACT ONE

Act Two

Not all the wisdom in old Bodley's books,
Their leather bindings, capitals of gold,
Crested and ranked like angels in grey dust
Row after row to reach eternity
Can buy one moment out of purgatory.
Only the pollen scent of innocence
Which cold and griping learnèd men greed for
A lifetime in their dens, but never find,
Lifts to the kiss of God : so Magdalene.
Tiberius, agèd and torn apart
By bursts of frenzied inactivity —
The wishes of Augustus still his law —
Heard that the cringing Senate had rejected
His great proposal for the Christians
(You'll find it all there in Tertullian)
Because they had not stamped their own approval
On the agenda first. So weak men cling
To rules to give them petty dignity.
Few understand the nature of true goodness,
Though nearly everyone can recognize
Good, and then, out of vested interest,
Reject it, plausibly; smile, and pass on.
Every imaginative probing of
The unknown transforms the known. Tiberius
In anger left Capri, made his way north
At last. The trembling Senate heard him reach
His villa within very sight of Rome.
God took his longing soul at Misenum.
When Caesar entered Rome, he was a corpse;
Followed by Satan's son, Caligula.

John, and our play, move on now, seventy years
To Ephesus, where the loved one of God,
Last eye-witness on earth, lives on : one hundred
Years of age, and failing fast, although
Fierce light of sanctity still burns his bones,
Refined now of its youthful motes, serene
And clear, ready to fly back to its source.
Go forth upon your journey, Christian soul!
Though not before the final act is played,
Your Gospel finished, and fresh men of God
Strengthened by beasts and fires of martyrdom
Are blest and guided on that pilgrimage
Down broken arches of the centuries
Into our present chaos, these last days
Before the final conflagration.
Trajan is Emperor. John, near his grave,
Completes his Gospel in a desert cave.

SCENE ONE

Near Ephesus

JOHN

This cool shade of the cave, this burning desert,
This Roman world so slow to learn the truth,
The way, the life . . . How can I with rough pens
And only parchment skins to write it down
Complete some memories of all he said
In that brief, perfect life once shared with me
So long ago? Days spent in hot Judaea,
Samaria, and dark Jerusalem,
City now utterly destroyed, her walls,
Her sanctuary battered down by Titus.
Now only Herod's empty towers stand :
Three monuments to Caesar's butchery.
All Jesus' closest friends are taken back
To God, save only me, last one on earth
Who shared his human thoughts and prayers;
    my Christ
With laughter, tears, and blessing on his lips;

Who skimped his meals, and would neglect his sleep.
When I am loved into eternal life
This last surviving link will be extinct —
Though only in the flesh! The Church moves on
As resurrected body of our Lord!
Now, on my hundredth birthday, I will spend
All the thin heat this body burns, to write.
'And John the Baptist said, "I am the voice
Of one that's crying in the wilderness
'Make straight the way of the Lord!' I am not fit
So much as to undo his shoelaces
Who is amongst you now. Why? I baptize
With water, but he shall baptize with fire.
Immeasurable distance separates
Pale onlooker from looked-at Light itself.
See! Now the sacrificial Lamb of God
In innocence and saddest gentleness
Lays down his life to clean the wickedness
Caused by us all in this our cruel world . . ." '
My ink's congealed. Alke! Please bring some fire
To melt it, or I'll use blood from my veins
To fix the memories omitted by
Mark, Luke, and Matthew, which will die with me
Lost, unrecorded, or in garbled fable
Tickle the ears of unbelieving smiles.
Alke! A girl, though young enough to be
My great-great-great-granddaughter, loved of God.
Burrhus and she guard me from Ephesus
In this my cave, until my days are done.

SCENE TWO

Enter ALKE

ALKE   Yes, here is fire. Didn't you hear me answer?
            My Father in God, they say you'll live for ever!

JOHN   No! That's a gross distortion of the truth!
            Because I'm old enough to be a legend
            That does not give me immortality

In any earthly sense : nor would I want it.
I long to be united now with God.
When Peter said to Jesus 'What of John?'
Jesus replied — these are his actual words :
'If I will that he stays here till I come,
Why, what is that to you?' He said it kindly
To emphasize Peter would follow him —
One day upon a cross, as we found, later :
Martyred, with our great Paul, by Nero's will.

ALKE   We shall be very lost when you are gone.

JOHN   Let not your heart be troubled, neither let
It be afraid. As you believe in God,
Believe me also when I tell you Jesus
Told us, and tells you, this : 'I have prepared
A place for you within my Father's house;
And if it were not so, I would have said.
If you shall ask anything in my name
I will do it. Only, keep my commandments,
And show you love me by your faithfulness.'

ALKE   Both Paul and Peter could face agony,
But I can't!

JOHN   Little one, may you be spared.

ALKE   They have not spared Ignatius. Now the news
Is he has been arrested and condemned.
My family back home in Smyrna talk
Of persecution across Antioch.
Here's Burrhus — he will tell you.

SCENE THREE

Enter BURRHUS

BURRHUS   Yes, their bishop,
'God's Fiery One', Ignatius of Antioch,
Theophorus as he's so often called,

Has been tried and condemned to the wild beasts
By Antioch's provincial magistrate,
A jumped-up, power-hungry sycophant,
Determined that Ignatius should return
To the bold paganism of his youth,
Or, in the Flavian amphitheatre,
Die feeding bloodlust of imperial Rome.

JOHN   Has he appealed to Caesar?

BURRHUS   Unlike Paul
He is not privileged with citizenship
Of Rome; only of Heaven. The very worst
The crowds demand : the cross, fire, savage beasts,
New horrors of the amphitheatre
Unthinkable to us, wait him in Rome.

JOHN   Then I must see him.

BURRHUS   He has now reached Smyrna
Where for a while he will remain; his guard
Have business there after the next assize.

JOHN   Burrhus, go to him. Take Onesimus,
Euplus, Crocus, and Fronto. You come from
        Smyrna,
Alke, and know it. Find them safe lodging there.
Tell Polycarp, that good and blessèd man,
The pastor of your Smyrnan church, I'll come
Myself. You first. All of us will support
Our own Ignatius in his martyrdom.

SCENE FOUR

Smyrna.

IGNATIUS   Yes, Polycarp. Ten of those savage leopards —
I mean ten Roman soldiers — are my gaolers.

POLYCARP   Ignatius, how can you endure their taunts,
Their casual bullying, their sadism?

IGNATIUS   They try to make me live up to my name
           And watch me lose my temper. It is hard.
           One of our golden-tongued brothers in Christ
           Called me 'A soul seething with divine eros',
           And they have jeered about it ever since.
           But, gentle Polycarp, we must put up
           With everything for God's sake; so that he
           May also endure us ! I am the least
           Of all the flock, the latest to the fold,
           Least worthy, and deserve all this, and more.
           Thank you for comforting me in your city
           Here. I have often longed to be with you
           In Smyrna. Now I am. My chains are jewels
           Whose preciousness has brought us face to face.

POLYCARP   (*Kissing* IGNATIUS'*s chains*)
           Father in God, our bishop of Antioch;
           I do not have your learning, nor your age,
           Experience, or sad predicament . . .

IGNATIUS   Sad? Yes! But never plead for my release.
           I am a convict. You, thank God, are free.
           Yet this entanglement in Satan's power
           Among the Roman eagles has led me
           Into the deep thoughts of our Jesus Christ.
           Even as I say this, oh! the devil laughs
           To hear me boast in spiritual pride.
           I have become afraid to hear the comfort
           Of those who tell me I shall win a crown
           Of martyrdom. Not that I fear to die,
           But compliments become a scourge to me
           Because they fan my impetuous ambition,
           And at the very moment I can see
           Armies of angels battlementing heaven
           And mighty Peter bending down his hand
           To lift me up to walk among the ranks
           That part and glitter in gold martyrs' crowns
           Above the principalities of God
           I choke and struggle and am thrust to hell
           Snatched at the height of joy. So bear with me.
           The truest consolation you can give
           Is gentleness in prayer for my pride.

POLYCARP   What of the friends who plead for your release?

IGNATIUS   This journey I am taking has begun
                  Well. I am prisoner of Jesus Christ,
                  Even as Paul, and many blessèd saints
                  Before me lead the way. What I fear most
                  Is not the cry the circling crowd applaud
                  In Rome, but generosity of friends
                  Who would prevent me dying like my Lord;
                  For I shall never have so clear a chance
                  To leap to God again.

POLYCARP   Your roots of faith are firm, and bear rich fruit
                  For our Lord Jesus Christ. We came with nothing
                  Into this world, and neither can we carry
                  Anything with us, save a perfect end
                  The consummation of a life of prayer.
                  Stand firm in your great passionate content;
                  Steadfast, immovable. And when you reach
                  The farther shore beyond the storm-wind's strength
                  Pray for us here below.

IGNATIUS   I will.

                              SCENE FIVE

                  Enter BURRHUS.

BURRHUS   Soft napkins
                  For the wounds your chains have worn.

IGNATIUS   Ah, Burrhus, Burrhus,
                  This God-loved deacon sent to me from John
                  In Ephesus has raised and refreshed my spirits.
                  I wish that everyone would be like him.

BURRHUS   What, your delightful gaolers?

POLYCARP   Burrhus, you have
                  The calm of spirit that Ignatius needs.

BURRHUS   No, I have nothing. All I've learned is John's.
              I care for him in his extreme old age
              With Alke, while he finishes his book
              Of Jesus' life and teachings; the last Gospel.

IGNATIUS   God will bless you for all that you are doing.

BURRHUS   You two are mighty men of God; but I
              Merely the messenger to say that John
              Is here to visit you; but first he must
              Comfort our sister in Christ, who comes before
              Pliny this afternoon, charged with the crime
              Of being an atheist, a Christian.

POLYCARP   Which sister in Christ?

BURRHUS   Flavia Domitilla.

IGNATIUS   Niece of the late Domitian, Emperor?
              Why is she here?

BURRHUS   She is a widow now,
              Her husband Flavius Clemens executed
              Although cousin to our late Emperor,
              And she has fled the Imperial Family.

IGNATIUS   My guards unlock the door. Kneel for my blessing,
              Young Polycarp. Your lack of Hebrew learning
              Protects your innocence. These shipwrecked times
              Demand a pilot in extremity
              Who has your gifts. Use all your energy
              To ferret out the faithful, each by name —
              And hold more services to strengthen them.
              Burrhus I hope will stay with me. All blessing.
              Pray for my church bereft in Antioch;
              Pray for the souls of all who suffer pain;
              And Polycarp, pray we may meet again
              In the great heart of Christ's eternity.

              Fade.

SCENE SIX

DOMITILLA   I feel at peace with you.

JOHN   You, too, have suffered.
              And, Domitilla, grief has made you strong.
              In worldly terms you have seen more than most :
              Your husband martyred, and your Rome estates
              First confiscated by Domitian,
              Then restored by good Nerva; now, once more
              In doubt because you harbour underground,
              In a fine double-crypted catacomb
              Bright with the frescoes of devoted ones,
              Our Christian family. God will reward,
              Protect, and bless you.

DOMITILLA   If I confess our faith,
              Then I'll betray those hiding in my grounds
              And they'll be caught.

JOHN   If we confess Christ he will stand by us.
              Witness is all.

DOMITILLA   John, what is Pliny like
              Now he has settled in Bithynia,
              And his wide jurisdiction reaches south
              As far as Ephesus?

JOHN   A thoughtful man.
              When Zosimus, his own freed slave, spat blood,
              He gave him money and wrote to a friend
              In Egypt to care for him in the sun,
              So air and milk of Africa might heal
              The wasting boy who played the lyre so well.
              He is not cruel, and indeed has written
              To Trajan to enquire what should be done
              With us.

DOMITILLA   And has the Emperor replied?

JOHN   No word has reached me.

DOMITILLA   I will ask him, then;
For others of the Imperial Family
Believe in Christ : we cannot all be killed,
Or Dido's pyre will reach Vesuvius!

JOHN   Yes; you and Pliny are patrician blood —
He will respect you; and you have my prayers.
If the world hates you, know it hated Christ.
But you are chosen for eternity.

DOMITILLA   Your time with me has helped. Lie in my room.
I never will forget your gentleness
With me today. There is the court-room bell.
In God's will, and your prayers, all may be well.

Exit JOHN.

SCENE SEVEN

Enter PLINY.

PLINY   Flavia Domitilla?

DOMITILLA   Pliny.

PLINY   Welcome.

DOMITILLA   Where is the court by which I must be tried?

PLINY   Flavia Domitilla, you will know
Our age demands the highest integrity
And standards of equity, and humanity,
In all procedures legal.

DOMITILLA   Does this mean
I am not to be tried; simply condemned?

PLINY   Imperial lady, no! It is decreed —
And rightly so in our enlightened age —
'Better a guilty person should go free

Than innocence mistakenly condemned
Tarnish the virtue of *res publica*.'
Your husband was the Consul, was he not?

DOMITILLA   He was.

PLINY   And cousin of Domitian, as are you?

DOMITILLA   I was Domitian's niece.

PLINY   Related twice
To him I served as prefect! Well. I too
Have lost an uncle. He was dear to me.
At Misenum, one August afternoon
He had been sunbathing; had a cold bath,
And started on his books, when my dear Mother
Drew his attention to a mushroom cloud
Dirty with soil and ashes, pumice-stone
And rubble from the mountain, rising high
Like a tall pine, fanning to cascade down.
He put his shoes on, called the warships out
And sailed to rescue friends across the bay.
As night fell, stark against the darkness, huge
Sheets of broad flame shot up at several points
Along the mountain. Wild and dangerous
Waves wrenched the battered boats. Everywhere
          smell
Of sulphur filled the nostrils. By the dawn,
Denser and blacker than night ever was,
Thick fumes had closed his windpipe. Two days later
He still looked more like sleep than death.
          I miss him.

DOMITILLA   I knew him as the Prefect of the fleet.

PLINY   You knew him? Well, well, well! Now, we must talk
A little of the charge anonymous
Which brings you here.

DOMITILLA   Anonymous?

PLINY   Yes, that
Is why no court is called. Merely examination
By me, in private, here.

DOMITILLA   I see. And why?

PLINY   Today, under great Trajan, no defendant
May be convicted merely on suspicion,
Accused anonymously. No. Those days,
Thank all the gods, are gone.
Now, Domitilla; take care what you say,
For no-one will convict you, but yourself.
Be wise, say nothing. Just observe the norms
Of sweet decorum and of common sense.
Let moderation be our guide in all,
And courtesy to our loved Emperor.

DOMITILLA   What must I do?

PLINY   Now, Domitilla, we
Should think a moment of why I am here.
We are patricians; I, as well as you.
We know the guardian of the Roman laws
And constitution, guarantor of peace
Throughout the world, Caesar, must hold the hearts
And minds of all; and all he asks of us,
The educated ruling class, is nominal
Allegiance. Mere good form unites us all,
And makes cohesive this great sprawling mass
We call the Empire.

DOMITILLA   Yes, I gladly give
To Caesar what is his.

PLINY   Good! Then that's settled.
The saving common sense of the true Roman.
And now — come. Will you dine with me?

DOMITILLA   Yes, Pliny
I think you studied under Quintilian?

PLINY   Why, yes I did! A wise, and humane man;
               Achieved the *ornamenta consularia*.

DOMITILLA   He did. My husband, Flavius, won that for him.
               Quintilian was tutor to our sons.

PLINY   Then we have much to talk of.

DOMITILLA   He would say
               In Cato's words, 'A good man, skilled in speaking,
               Does not disguise the truth but looks for it.'
               Pliny, I am a Christian.

PLINY   Domitilla! . . .
               Now come to dinner and forget all this.
               Caesar's our lord, we have agreed. The form
               Of courtesy is all that I require.

DOMITILLA   Yes, I agree. But I am still a Christian.

PLINY   Now please don't ruin all that I have done.
               Honour great Caesar; and don't rock the boat.
               Back the Establishment, and the Establishment
               Will cover you. Now; Roman law requires,
               Demands the self-accused be asked three times.
               I will postpone your second thirty days.
               Say nothing more of this.

DOMITILLA   I will not change.
               To Caesar I give Caesar's, but to Christ
               Alone I give the honour due to God.

PLINY   Go out from here! I will not listen! You
               Have lost a first-class dinner. Jupiter!
               Why can't you see I've done the best I can
               By you? In thirty days we'll meet again.
               For God's sake find some sense!

DOMITILLA   I will.

PLINY   Good-bye!

Fade.

SCENE EIGHT

IGNATIUS   O dearest John!

JOHN   God-carried Ignatius, you
                Whom as a babe Jesus held in his arms;
                I'll simply tell you what our Peter said:
                'Belovèd, do not think the fiery trial
                Which is to come to you is strange, unseen
                Of God. Rather rejoice that when his glory
                Shall be revealed, you share his sufferings
                And will be glad with an exceeding joy.'
                Do you remember?

IGNATIUS   Yes. O John, guide me!
                I am God's wheat, ground fine between the teeth
                Of wild beasts to become pure bread for Christ.
                I want no more of what these men call life,
                For I would rather die than rule the earth.
                John, what is this I feel? What is this weird
                Joy the arena beasts bring out in me?
                I hope they will leap on, and tear, and not
                Hang back, as some do, in their fear of man.
                If so, I'll coax, entice them, violently,
                If necessary to feed on my flesh.
                Now I begin to feel myself our Lord's.
                May nothing come between me and my God.
                Come fire, nailed crucifixion, savage beasts,
                Pain wrenching out my bones, hacking of limbs,
                Crushing my entire body head to foot,
                The gladiator's butchery, come all
                The devil can provide, only give me
                A chance to win through to my Jesus Christ.

JOHN   My son; he said: 'He that believes in me
                The works that I do, he will also do

And greater works than these, because I go
Back to my Father to prepare a place
For you with God. And I will pray my Father
That he will send the Comforter to be
Your strength; and on that great day you will know
That I am in my Father, you in me,
And I in you.'

SCENE NINE

POLYCARP *thrown in, in chains.*

IGNATIUS   Polycarp!

POLYCARP   They'll fetch you now!

JOHN   Son Polycarp; you I ordained bishop. (*Pause*)
         We three will soon meet, raised by Christ through
                 death.
         These words of his must be my parting gift :
         'Peace I leave with you. My peace give to you.
         Not as the world gives do I give it you.'
         I will not say much more. The Prince of Darkness
         Comes. Simply this : 'Let not your heart be troubled,
         Neither let it be afraid.
         In the world tribulation shall be ours :
         But triumph — Christ has overcome the world.'

         Blackout.

SCENE TEN

PLINY   Nicetes, I am glad to see you here
         On this day dedicated to great Caesar.
         (Also, I learn, the Hebrew feast of Purim,
         Their Greater Sabbath.) You will attend the games
         That celebrate our Caesar's deity.
         Will your young sister soon be joining us?

NICETES Pliny, I am uneasy. Alke has run
         To Ephesus, and may soon be sucked dry

Of Roman virtue by the Christians.
I hate them. Atheists! They undermine
Time-honoured customs, and are arrogant.
They break up families — no, not just mine —
And everyone that comes within their power's
Corrupted. God knows what their secrets are
When they forgather at the break of day
To cannibalize bread with human flesh.

PLINY   You hear the crowds? The citizens are pleased.
Today our public entertainment will
Hold nothing lax to weaken or destroy
Their manly spirits, but will teach them strength;
Inspire each one to look with scorn on death;
To bear with patience honourable wounds;
. And understand, even through criminals
And slaves, the stoic impassivity
That made us masters of the whole known world.

NICETES   There is no finer testing of a boy
Than showing him the gladiators' games
(Yes. As I take my own son Herodes)
And training him to be unmoved by blood.

PLINY   With the exception of the Amisenes,
The Emperor will not permit unlicensed
Gatherings. You say the Christians still meet?
If they are dangerous, if they become
Political societies that swear
To overthrow the State, I shall be firm,
Nicetes. But in fact, all I have found
By torture of two slave-girls, deaconesses
They call them, is wholly commendable.
They take an oath never to rob or steal,
To hate adultery, and to pay debts.
They sing to Christ as if he were a god,
And eat some harmless, ordinary food
Together.

NICETES   But they break up loyalties!

PLINY   Just one more cult; degenerate, no doubt;
                 Extravagant, the lengths they take it to,
                 But little more. However, you shall see.
                 We have one legal hearing to complete
                 Before the games begin and I take up
                 That seat in Trajan's name, the accolade
                 And homage of the seething Smyrnaeans.

NICETES   Good!

PLINY   Send us in the Christian Polycarp!

Enter POLYCARP.

NICETES   Why, you!

POLYCARP   Nicetes, I am glad to see you.

PLINY   Now, Polycarp. We do not have much time.
                 You are a scholar, and respected here;
                 And, just to make sure all I do is right,
                 I've corresponded with the Emperor
                 About fair treatment of you Christians.

POLYCARP   And what is his reply?

PLINY   I'll read it you.
                 Nicetes, kiss the seal imperial!
                 Now listen. 'My dear Pliny, you are right
                 In your discussion of the Christians.
                 There is no general rule. Don't hunt them out;
                 But if they come before you, and the charge
                 Is proved against them, punish them; however,
                 If one denies he is a Christian,
                 And offers prayers once more to our gods,
                 You are to pardon him, no matter how
                 Suspect his past may be. Do not accept
                 Anonymous informers : such are out
                 Of keeping with the spirit of this age.'
                 A wise and sane approach!

NICETES
                                        Look, Polycarp.
What harm is there in saying Caesar's lord
And throwing incense in this statue's flame?
(*Nicetes throws a pinch of incense in the flame*)
Kyrios Caesar! Dominus Traianus!

Answering cry comes from crowd.

PLINY
We must walk in now to the theatre.
You see the crowds? Look. Swear by Caesar's
        genius
And I shall let you go and set you free.

NICETES
(*Pause*) Curse Christ.

POLYCARP
                (*Stung*) These many years I've honoured him
And he has never done me any wrong.
How can I possibly blaspheme my King
Who saved me?

NICETES
                                Take the oath!

PLINY
                                        Come; simply say
'Away with atheists!' to all this crowd.

POLYCARP
(*Looks at the audience*) 'Away with atheists!'

PLINY
                                Good! Take the oath
        To Caesar. Hold this incense.

NICETES
                                Play the man.

POLYCARP
If you believe that I will go against
My conscience, and swear that Caesar's God,
Then you pretend you do not know me. I,
As you well know, am and will die a Christian.
But if you wish to learn just what we teach,
Appoint a day, and give me Roman hearing.

PLINY
You have that hearing, now. Persuade the crowd!

POLYCARP   You I respect, as honourable, worthy,
                Chosen by God as ruler over us;
                And we are taught to give you due respect
                If it does not conflict with our beliefs.
                But as for these, a circus audience
                Restless with lust for blood is not a mob
                Appropriate to hear defence in Christ.

PLINY   I have wild beasts, and I shall throw you to them
                Unless you change your mind.

POLYCARP   To change from truth
                To lies is not acceptable to us.

PLINY   If you despise the beasts, then I have fire!

POLYCARP   Your fire burns but a moment; then goes out.
                But each of us one day shall stand before
                The judgement seat of Christ; and everyone
                Who has disowned him, or reneged, will burn
                In everlasting punishment of fire
                Nothing can quench. Come! Why do you delay?

NICETES   (*Announces to crowd*)
                Hear! Polycarp confesses he's a Christian!
                Polycarp confesses he's a Christian!

CROWD   *Christianos ad leones! Christianos ad leones!*

PLINY   Have we a lion to let loose on him?

NICETES   The beast sports that have kept the crowd amused
                Till our arrival are concluded, and
                The animals returned back to their cages.

CROWD   Burn him! Burn him! Burn him! Burn him!
                     Burn him!

PLINY   Because you will not regulate your life
                By Caesar, and acknowledge him as God,
                But stubborn to futility persist

In worshipping your Christ, to the exclusion
Of elementary Roman sanity;
Because you will not take one pinch of incense
And throw it in the flame before this statue,
But proud beyond belief challenge the State
And prove to be subversive with contempt,
You, and eleven others here, shall die
By fire on this high Roman holiday.
Go! Tell the crowd that they shall have their will!
You might have lived. And Caesar is God, still.

SCENE ELEVEN

Ephesus

JOHN *has fallen asleep over the parchment on his*
lap.

BURRHUS   Yes, he seems fragile and eats little.

ALKE   Scarcely
              Enough to keep his energy alive.

BURRHUS   How has he been while I have been away?

ALKE   The journey north, the trial of Domitilla,
              The arrest of those in her Rome catacomb,
              Of Polycarp, and many others too,
              Was more than age and horseback could endure.
              His hundred years can carry grief a little
              Longer, but not much. I stayed on in Smyrna
              In the cold hope my family might try
              To understand the loving word of God.

BURRHUS   What did they say? Have they forgiven you?

ALKE   They hate Christ with a fierce implacable
              Insistence that is madness; say he has
              Destroyed our family, split us apart:
              And if I do not sacrifice to Caesar,
              They, even little Herodes, will make

The great propraetor use his bed of shells
To torture and compel me to recant.

JOHN   (*Slowly*) You think your family will Judas you?
Alke, come here. God has decreed you shall not
Have to endure torture. There is an island
Shaped like a horse's head and neck; just three
Volcanic mountains, like the Trinity.
It's very small, and very beautiful.
The waves around it are a sea of glass,
And from the mountains, light divides the world
As you look down. The walls are black, like jasper,
The city gold, brighter than chrysolite;
The streets are clear as pearl, and the swift stream
Brighter than diamonds left in the sun.
It was a penal colony of Rome,
Then left deserted. Now, our Christian refuge.
I have a son in God who bears my name;
There he will honour you in his old age
As I have done — and you must care for him
For he, too, has a mighty book to write.

ALKE   Through you I'm happy. But you seem to be
Preparing us for days when you are gone?

JOHN   I am. My work on earth is nearly done.
Burrhus, if any part of this our Gospel
On which I have been working seems unfinished,
You, who know all my literary thoughts,
And Alke, you who know what I would write,
Complete and tidy it. Mankind still craves
For books they can think sacred. Look what Greeks
Have done to Homer — allegorized bloodshed.
The Jews, too. In my Gospel all is there
The intellect of man can wrestle with;
For guided by the Holy Spirit I
Have told his doctrine of divine compassion
Through allegories, juxtapositionings,
Statements, exempla — with severe restraint.
Yes! Even Pliny and Quintilian
Might nod in our direction. But we speak

For centuries to come. Thousands of years
From now, perhaps, some distant northern island
On the far limit wall of Empire,
Rome's farthest outpost, will repeat these words
And be brought home to Christ. Burrhus, tell me
The news you bring of our Ignatius.

BURRHUS   I joined Ignatius, as you know, in Smyrna,
And both our friends from here in Ephesus
And also our host Smyrnaeans themselves
Urged me to go with him until he looked
His first on the shores of Europe. So I did;
Then left him. But while we had nights and days
In Troas, just before we parted, he
Dictated letters to me for the flock :
To those we left behind in Smyrna, and
Another to the Philadelphians.
I think there was one more he wished to write,
To Polycarp, but ships embarked, and soldiers
Took him away. His faith in God is strong.
God's carrier, indeed. May God lift him.

ALKE   (*To John*) You have not cried till now. I'll dry
                    your tears.

JOHN   Alke; tell me the worst — how Polycarp
Met God.

ALKE   He was condemned to burn before the crowds,
With twelve, I think, from Philadelphia
Who also stood firm and would not curse Christ.
Orthodox Jews in Smyrna hate us more
Than most, because our teaching supersedes
The Pentateuch. They rushed, with others too,
Collecting wood and kindling from the baths
And workshops. He took off his bloodstained clothes
Down to his waist; tried to undo his shoes,
But was too weak — and stood inside the circle,
His back against the stake. They locked the irons
Around him, but when nails were to be hammered
Into his limbs, he said 'You have no need
To nail me. God, who helps us to endure

The fire will also help me to remain
Here at the stake unmoved.' And so they spared
     him;
Tied him instead. Yes, like some noble ram
From a great flock offered in sacrifice.
He prayed — I could not hear now — then the
     flames
Blazed up. But God was kind. The hasty
     faggots
Encircling him drew air up in the centre
And no flames burned him. Like a vaulted chamber,
Or a ship's sail filled out with wind, the fire
Curved round. It was a miracle. A sweet
Scent rose up from the woodsmoke. Flames died
     down
And he was still unharmed. They called the man
Employed to give the coup de grâce to beasts
In the arena, the confector, who
Had not gone home yet though his work was done.
Grumbling, he came out with his new-cleaned knife
And stabbed our perfect martyr Polycarp.
The blood poured down extinguishing what little
Fire was left. (*Weeps*)

JOHN   You need tell me no more.

ALKE   I'm sorry. But the hardest part for me
Was that my brother made impossible
Our burial of his body; with a sneer
That Polycarp might rise as well, and we
Would worship Polycarp instead of Christ.

BURRHUS   What then?

ALKE   They burned him, and we have his
     bones.

JOHN   He wins the crown of immortality.
Ignatius, too. May the Almighty God
And Saviour of our souls, with all the saints
Rejoice above. Now. Bring two baskets with you,
And shovels.

SCENE TWELVE

Beyond the cave.

JOHN   Here, Burrhus, dig. And Alke, take the soil
In baskets while I pray. This is the last
Burden that I shall be to you, my children.
Dig ! Dig a secure trench.

*They mime the digging and uncover the coffin,
which is to be thought of as the trench.*

O God my Father
The hour is come. Thank you that my long life
Shared in the early days with your own Son
Ends in the glory of your spreading word.
The work is finished you gave me to do,
And I pray for those you have given me
And, beyond them, the martyrs and the saints
Both dead and living children of your joy.
As you sent me out to the world, so I
Pray you will sanctify their lives and minds
Through Jesus Christ our Lord. Your word is truth
And it will triumph through the universe.
Father, I commend, into your hands, my spirit.

*JOHN climbs into coffin. It is raised up and carried
out by four male figures. MARY VIRGIN, in full white
bridal dress, and holding a single lit candle, follows,
some way behind coffin, alone. Music for this
procession (during which the lights dim down to
only the candle) Allegri's Miserere (Psalm 51) for
Tenebrae, beginning with the second half of verse
one: 'According to the multitude of thy mercies . . .'
and closing at the end of verse six, or verse ten.
The soaring voice of the solo boy should be heard
in pitch darkness, after the candle held by the bride
has departed.*

END

Beyond the History Books to Eternity

Brian G. Cooper's review of Moving Reflections.

(THE STAGE, 9.ix.82)

Oxford University Players' première of 'Moving Reflections', Francis Warner's powerful new play on the life of St John of the Fourth Gospel, is a noteworthy event. As one would expect from this playwright, whose trilogy 'Requiem' on the Fringe in the early seventies aroused much critical attention, this is a profound and disturbing play, which takes the audience deep into the anguished, questing soul of that first-century world.

Guy Andrews' staging, characterized by an essential simplicity and economy of presentation, is effective. The sustained strength of the production is heightened by David Colmer's imaginative lighting of confined space to intensify the mood; and the philosophical-cum-theological dialogues, unfamiliar to the ears of our secular, post-Christian age, hold our close attention throughout.

The play is in two acts, the first set at the time of Jesus' death and resurrection, the second some 70 years later with the death of St John. The gospel writer, strongly played by Jeremy Davies, is portrayed biblically as the adopted son of Mary the Virgin, from whom he learns so much. The only humorous scene in Act One is where they joyfully debate various drafts of his First Epistle : Mary arguing for a simple, loving message, John more worried about the complexities of human waywardness.

Reclusive Tiberius, played by Brett Hannam, alternatively imperious and anguished, rules Rome with one eye beyond the history books to eternity, ready for debate with Philo the philosopher and open to the new Christian message of young Mary Magdala (Caroline Thomas) — their meeting is the play's most memorable sequence.

The second act sees centenarian John completing his 'Golden Book' amid violence and persecution. Francis Warner uses proper poetic licence to bring the latter event to the close of the first century, but for the most part adheres to history and the pseudo-history of hagiography.

But this is not religious documentary theatre, but a poetic exploration, in blank verse, of a towering Christian and literary genius, whose life and times have a haunting and evocative relevance to our own anguished age. By never descending to the didactic, Francis Warner has given us a memorable play of profound content and singular immediacy.